My Personal Picture Album

Dale Evans Rogers

OLIPHANTS

OLIPHANTS

Marshall, Morgan & Scott Limited
Blundell House
Goodwood Road, London S.E. 14 6BL

Copyright © 1971   by Fleming H. Revell Company
Printed in the United States of America

ISBN 0 551 00219 0

CONTENTS

Hello! I'm Dale Evans Rogers.

It's often said that one picture is worth ten thousand words. That has always struck me as something of an exaggeration, but pictures do illustrate and clarify the meaning of almost any subject you can think of.

This was brought home to me in a very real way after the publication of my book *The Woman at the Well* in 1970. After reading it, quite a few people were kind enough to write and tell me how much they enjoyed it, and some said it had helped them face their problems with new courage. But several also mentioned that they wished the book had contained more pictures.

In response to these comments, my publisher, the Fleming H. Revell Company, suggested that I put out a book completely given over to pictures — my own "photo album" that would actually show some of the experiences I've had as I traveled along life's adventurous road. *Dale — My Personal Picture Album* is the result of that suggestion. I hope you enjoy it.

Here, pull your chair a little closer and we'll go through the book together. As you look at the pictures, I'll explain a little about each one.

Growing Up

As a small child, my mother says, I was quite vain and pirouetted in front of a mirror when someone gave me new clothes. I also was ready to pose for the camera. I was never too busy posing, though, to enjoy a lively romp with my brother, Hillman. Thinking of all the hours I've spent on horseback, this picture—made at Grandfather's ranch—seems prophetic!

New hairdo, new dress . . . Now thirteen, and feeling quite grown-up, here I am with my first permanent and my first formal party dress. It had a pouf of real ostrich feathers and had belonged to my Aunt Rose. When I put it on, I *really* felt grown-up.

Boys fascinated me, as they fascinate most adolescent girls. My family often laughed at my performance with the boys, but I felt that I was fully capable of coping with the opposite sex. When my parents tried to divert my interest, to prolong my enjoyment of childhood until I was a little more mature, I was resentful and began to strain at the leash.

I loved to dance—although it was frowned upon by our church—and I longed to attend the public dances. "Everybody in town" was there, I told my mother. Finally, I talked her into acting as one of the chaperones for younger girls who were too young to date. Naturally, this meant I could go along, and before long I was dancing every dance.

Within a year, I met my first steady, a boy in his late teens from a neighboring town. He soon became my husband, and father to my son Tom.

The Lonely Struggle

I grew up fast!

Still in my teens, with my marriage on the rocks, I had to find a way to support myself and Tommy; so I enrolled in a business school.

I was terribly alone—alone in the sense of having full responsibility for myself and my baby, but also in a deeper sense: Although I had grown up in a Christian home, I lacked any real commitment to Christ.

If I had turned to God when my marriage failed and asked Him *then* to straighten out the mess I had made of my life, things might have been different. But I thought I could make it on my own. In fact, I made a pact with myself to be completely independent in my scramble to climb to the top.

This picture was taken in Memphis, Tennessee, where I went to work for an insurance firm. After hours (and sometimes even on the job) I wrote songs and dreamed of becoming a singer.

One day my boss asked me if I could accompany myself on the piano; if so, he thought he could get me on as a guest on a radio program in which he had a sponsor's interest.

The next Friday night Frances Fox made her radio debut, playing and singing "Mighty Lak a Rose." Then, to my unbounded joy, the station offered me a regular spot.

In those days, people would listen to you sing. Listeners phoned in requests, and I would play and sing as many songs as I could during the 30-minute show.

Civic organizations began inviting me to sing at luncheons and banquets. Occasionally, the pay was in real money (as much as twenty dollars); but mostly it was chicken croquettes and peas. Anyway, the experience was good. Within a few months I had moved up from that first small radio station to the most powerful one in Memphis. When the big dance bands came to town, I would be on hand, with an escort, and sometimes they would ask me to sing a number. My name began to get up there in popular demand.

In Louisville, Kentucky, where this picture was made, I landed my first job with really good pay.

The program director at Station WHAS gave me my professional name, Dale Evans, when I joined the staff. It was designed primarily for easy pronunciation by announcers (it rolls off the tongue smoothly) and is almost impossible to mispronounce or misspell.

I was one of the featured singers at WHAS, singing pop music — things like "Shine On, Harvest Moon."

14

After a terrible scare, when it seemed that Tommy might have contracted polio, we went back to the Texas farm.

It was a real relief for me to know that my boy was safe and happy. How he loved that farm and the small-town life that went with it! He fairly bubbled with joy and bloomed with good health.

But I knew I had to find work; I couldn't let my parents support us indefinitely. I found a job on the staff of Station WFAA, in Dallas, as the band singer on a popular program called "The Early Birds."

This picture was taken on the bank of Turtle Creek, in Dallas. It was a publicity shot for WFAA.

A pianist and orchestral arranger I had known in Louisville came to play the piano and do arrangements for the WFAA staff band. We had dated frequently in Louisville, and our dates began again. A year later, we were married.

For a while, I sang with Herman Walman's Orchestra. Usually, we appeared in rented auditoriums for dances. We did some theaters, too, but mostly one-night stands, starting about nine and closing at one.

This is the picture we used for publicity.

After two more years in Dallas, we went to Chicago. I got a job as a jazz singer with an orchestra at the Edgewater Beach Hotel. Anson Weeks, whose orchestra was playing at the Aragon Ballroom, was looking for a female vocalist, and I got the job. The next year was a kaleidoscope of dance band one-nighters and hotel engagements. Often, we had to drive hundreds of miles from date to date.

I finally left the band because Tom was ready for junior high school and I wanted him with me.

There was an opening on the staff of WBBM (CBS network). An audition got it for me. I did about six regular shows a week. In those days, everything was done live; there was no such thing as going back and saying, "Well, I goofed; I'd like to pick it up there."

publicity
shot
for
B.S.
Biro

This photograph, taken in 1940, was a publicity shot for my own CBS show, "That Gal from Texas." I sang and talked and announced my own songs. About a third of the songs were Mexican or Spanish (which I learned phonetically). In Texas there is quite a bit of Mexican music because it's a border state. (The sombrero is one I picked up in Mexico when I was there with the Anson Weeks band.)

At the same time I was working at WBBM, I sang every night at the Blackstone, Sherman, or Drake Hotel, and finally I reached the top spot — the then-famous Chez Paree Supper Club. At last, the breaks seemed to be coming my way.

Now Tom and I went to church regularly. Somehow, although I had no solid relationship with the Lord, I wanted my child to have what I lacked.

The minister made me uncomfortable with his references to "the claims of Jesus Christ." Often, I would feel myself drawn toward the Cross, but later I would rationalize my feelings of guilt for not coming out boldly for Christ and for not walking in His way. I was terribly afraid that He might require something that would cost too much — something that would perhaps jeopardize my career. My greatest goal was to make a name for myself in show business. I felt I *had* to make a lot of money so that I could guarantee Tom's future — a college education and everything else that money could buy for him.

I was torn between my desire to be a good housekeeper, wife, and mother and my consuming ambition as an entertainer. It was like trying to ride two horses at once, and I couldn't seem to control either one of them.

Camellia
House
Drake Hotel
1940

One day I received an unexpected telegram that was to change the course of my life. It was from a Hollywood agent who had heard me sing. He wanted to see some photographs of me, with a view to a possible screen test.

I had no desire to go to Hollywood. Besides, I was fully aware of some hard, cold facts: I wasn't an actress; I didn't think I was pretty enough to be in pictures; and I was twenty-eight years old. So I paid no attention to the telegrams, but they kept coming. Finally, I had a talk with my program director. He advised me to play along and see what would happen.

The screen test at Paramount Studios was being conducted to find an ingenue lead for a picture starring Bing Crosby and Fred Astaire—*Holiday Inn*. When they found I couldn't dance, I was disqualified, but they decided to go ahead and make the screen test, just in case there might be a chance at something else.

I went back to Chicago after the test, back to the old routine. My heart was still set on New York, not Hollywood, and I almost put the whole affair out of my mind. Then a call from the agent, Mr. Rivkin, informed me that Hollywood was still there, beckoning. He said that Paramount had not taken up its option on me, but Twentieth Century-Fox wanted me for a one-year contract. The salary would be four hundred dollars a week.

After all of our lean years, four hundred dollars looked like a lot of money. The whole family discussed the offer, pro and con, and decided that the answer ought to be yes.

In due time, the studio assigned me a part, a starring role in a college musical, *Campus in the Clouds*. I forgot my earlier reservations about film work; if I wasn't actually in the clouds, I was at least walking on air! But my joy was short-lived. When World War II broke out, the picture was shelved. All I could do then was mark time and wait for another break.

At about this time, I began to be painfully aware of a deep emptiness in my life. I had a Hollywood contract and a good income, but nothing satisfied me or gave me any sense of security.

My husband, his parents, Tom, and I attended church every Sunday, but even that didn't seem to help because I always left my faith on the church steps after the service.

The Hollywood Victory Committee called and asked me to entertain U. S. troops at USO shows. I did a lot of shows for the boys in army camps. My husband went with me when he could, accompanying me on the piano and doing spot jobs, but a lot of the time we went our separate ways, and we saw less and less of each other.

That's the way it is in Hollywood. In arranging schedules, family life isn't considered—you simply go where you have to go and do what you have to do without regard for the convenience of husband, wife, or children. We were making good money, but . . .

Then my contract came up for renewal. I had had only two small parts in pictures, and I began to worry. Sure enough, I found that the contract would not be renewed.

I asked my agent, Joe Rivkin, to suggest an agent who could help me get back into radio. He suggested a man named Art Rush.

Art steered me to NBC, where they were auditioning for "The Chase and Sanborn Hour," starring Edgar Bergen. I got the job.

It was wartime, and during those years I did almost six hundred shows for the USO and the Hollywood Victory Committee.

One of the songs I sang on almost every show was a number I wrote myself called "Will You Marry Me, Mr. Laramie?" It was cute, tasteful, and subtle. When I came out for my opening song, I would always survey the audience, looking for a very bashful serviceman. Then I would call him up to the stage and propose to him in this song.

This picture was taken at Fort Bliss, in El Paso, on one of the USO tours.

"Swing your Partner!!" — Republic

I was on "The Chase and Sanborn Hour" forty-three weeks, and I worked harder than hard. Everything seemed to be going well until I did something that, by show business standards, could be considered a fatal mistake. One of the network's top executives asked me to meet him in New York, and I refused. Before long I was dropped from the show. Since the season had already begun, there was no chance of getting another commercially sponsored program that year.

I needed help, but when I turned to my agent, Art Rush, I found that he had other things on his mind. In fact, he was just leaving for New York to see his number one client, a fast-rising singing cowboy named Roy Rogers.

With my whole career in jeopardy, my agent was leaving town to spend time with a star who already had it made! I exploded, and I informed Mr. Rush that since he obviously didn't have time for both me and that cowboy, I would find myself a new agent who could devote more time to my career. I left him and signed with Danny Winkler.

Danny got me a year's contract with Republic Studios. Two weeks later, I started a picture for Republic. It was called *Swing Your Partner*, a country musical with Lulu Belle and Scotty ("National Barn Dance") and Vera Vague ("Bob Hope Show").

Near the end of the first year at Republic, I took time off for a tour of the Texas army and air bases.

This picture shows a visit to boys on bivouac, high on a mountain in Texas. The head scarf was to protect my ears from the wind. The day before, I had been in bed with a strep throat, and I was shot full of medication. I sang for about forty-five minutes with no microphone, standing on top of a jeep.

I enjoyed the tours, and I liked the thought that I could help bring a little sunshine into the hearts of the soldiers. But today I realize that something vital was missing. Sadly, I now see that this was a rare opportunity to transmit a little spiritual awareness and hope. But since I had no spiritual conviction at the time, I couldn't share it with anyone else.

Enter Roy Rogers

One day, Herbert J. Yates, the boss at Republic, called me up to the front office. He had seen the musical *Oklahoma* and wanted to apply the same treatment to a new kind of Western. He wanted me as the leading lady. The male star would be — who else? Roy Rogers! I wasn't sure I wanted this part. Although I loved Westerns, and had always loved cow-pokes and horses, I had never thought of myself doing Western films. Besides, my ambition was still to get into a big, sophisticated musical.

Mr. Yates was sure I was the one for the part; so I did the picture. It was called *The Cowboy and the Senorita*. Roy was the cowboy, and I was a Mexican girl named Isabel Martinez.

Everyone took it for granted that I — a good Texan — knew how to ride a horse. Actually, I hadn't been on horseback since I was seven years old. I didn't even know which side to get on or how to hold the reins. Roy was incredulous, but I laughed it off, saying, "It's been a long time since Texas."

From the very beginning, I liked Roy Rogers. There was nothing phony about him. He dared to be himself and was as comfortable to have around as an old shoe. I enjoyed working with him.

The work itself wasn't easy, though. I thought I would never learn how to handle a horse. One day, riding at a canter down a steep slope, I bounced around so hard that the temporary caps flew off my teeth. To this day, I don't know how I stayed on that horse, and I thought I'd never get him to stop. When he finally came to a standstill, Roy walked over and said, "Well, I never saw so much sky between a woman and a horse in all my born days." He suggested that I take some riding lessons — that is, if I wanted to stay alive!

In spite of the problems, that first picture was a success, and I was immediately cast with Roy in another one. I usually played a reporter, or kind of a smart-alecky girl. I think the fans enjoyed watching me because they liked to hate me.

This photograph is a scene from a movie called *Lights of Old Santa Fe*. Roy is riding behind me, ribbing me about the city. (I'm sitting quite tall in the saddle, you'll notice.)

This shot is from a picture called *Song of Nevada* that Roy and I did in the middle forties.

Between shots on location, we had a lot of time to talk, and he began to get into my heart.

For one thing, he loved kids. When he would climb down from the saddle to talk to some little crippled boy or girl, there was no show about it; he meant it. I think the fact that we were both so fond of children was the first real bond of common interest between us.

Roy's lack of egotism also impressed me. He never really believed he could act. In fact, he didn't even think of himself as a particularly good singer, although he actually did sing well.

On screen or off, Roy was always himself. He was number one at the box office, but he was also the boy next door, a breath of clean country air, a handsome, two-fisted man sitting easy in his saddle.

Everyone who worked with Roy seemed to fall under his spell, and I was no exception.

When we finished a picture, we had to go to the still gallery, where publicity shots were taken for exhibitors to use in publicizing the picture. This is a publicity still for one of our pictures.

Here is a publicity shot for another picture we made, *San Fernando Valley*, a modern Western.

Before I realized what was happening, I had filmed nine Westerns, and it was clear to me then that I was being typed as a Western player. But I wasn't satisfied to be just a part of a team. I wanted to star, and I was convinced that a woman could go just so far in Westerns; it was not the leading lady but the handsome cowboy who always held the spotlight.

In each of my pictures, I worked hard to improve my performance. At the end of the workday, I would study the rushes of the previous day's filming, examining every gesture, movement, and expression—anything that could possibly be improved. When I went to bed at night, I was still thinking about it.

My self-interest and my drive to succeed grew until they threatened to crowd everything else from my life. An inflated ego is a very real hazard in show business. It can easily distort one's entire life. And that is what was happening to me. Of course, I couldn't see it then, but now I know that my insatiable ambition was demanding that I sacrifice the most precious things in life — love, marriage, and children.

As I rose in my career, my marriage declined. My husband and I were on opposite sides of the merry-go-round. He was a night person, working in the late afternoons and evenings. His social life came in the small hours of the morning. But I often had to get up at 4:30 A.M. I would work until seven or eight in the evening and fall into bed, exhausted, right after dinner. My husband was a fine, talented man, and I shall forever be grateful to him for his help and encouragement, but we had no life together.

If I had quit making pictures and directed more effort toward trying to make a home, perhaps it would have worked out. But it never occurred to me that I might give up my precious job. It was the fault of neither of us and both of us and of the relentless system to which we sold ourselves. This was Hollywood, and we were caught up in a typical Hollywood tragedy. In 1945 we were divorced.

Here I am on a horse that was trained to sit down. The picture was *Sunset in Eldorado*. It was shot in Las Vegas in 1946.

I had taken a few riding lessons in self-defense. Roy gave me some pointers, too. He showed me how to "take the action" in my knees and forelegs and how to lean back when I was pulling my horse to a stop. That was especially good to know, because I usually seemed to draw horses with the disposition of a convict breaking out of jail!

This is a press photo, showing Roy meeting me at the plane when I flew in for a rodeo.

At about this time, tragedy struck Roy's life. His wife, Arlene Wilkins, had given birth to a baby boy. With two girls already, Roy was overjoyed. They named the child Roy, Jr., and nicknamed him Dusty. The birth was by Caesarian section. Eight days later Arlene developed a blood clot and died.

Seeing Roy's stricken face, my troubles suddenly seemed insignificant.

Overnight, Roy's life turned into a nightmare. When he was working on a picture, the hours were unbelievably long. Then, as soon as it was finished, he would take off on a round of personal appearance tours; he needed the extra money for publicity, wardrobe, and the care of his children. His salary was small, considering the fact that he was a top box office attraction. He even had to pay the bills involved in answering his fan mail, which poured in from everywhere, with absolutely no help from the studio. And on top of all that, he had to think about running a home. He managed to find a series of nurses and housekeepers and companions for the children, but it was a rough road.

Roy and I were together most of our waking hours, and our attraction for one another grew. We had a rapport born of years of struggle in our work, and we felt completely at home with each other.

But when it came to marriage, neither of us wanted to rush into it. The question in both of our minds was: Would it work? I had tried marriage and struck out; I didn't want a third failure. Roy had his family to think about; marriage meant that I would become a part of that family. Could I adjust to the children, and could they adjust to me? What about discipline? As a child, I had resented correction. And I remembered my indignation at the correction of my own son, now grown, by others. Roy had never made any profession of Christian faith, and I had no really personal relationship with Christ; so there was no real help from religion for either of us.

Problems, problems, problems!

Late in the fall of 1947, when we were sitting on our horses in the chutes of a rodeo at the Chicago Stadium waiting to be announced, Roy asked me, "What are you doing New Year's Eve?"

I had no plans for New Year's Eve, which was a long time away.

"Well, then, why don't we get married?" he asked.

And so, on the last day of the year, we began our new life together.

As a child in Uvalde, Texas, I used to sit on the bank of the Nueces River and dream that some day I would marry Tom Mix. Every Saturday afternoon in Osceola, Arkansas, I watched old Tom and his horse and all but worshiped them. As it turned out, I came pretty close to my dream, didn't I?

Our Children

From the beginning, children were a vital part of our household; altogether, we had nine! Let me introduce them to you . . .

This is Tom on his wedding day, with Roy. Tom always thought a great deal of Roy, and Roy has admired Tom for the person he is, the character and ambition he has, and the faithful way he has served God.

The wedding was at the Fountain Avenue Baptist Church, with Linda and Cheryl as junior bridesmaids. Most of our family came from Texas and Arkansas, and I wept when I looked at Tom and Barbara standing there side by side.

Their marriage was made in heaven. Both were committed Christians. If I had been asked to handpick a wife for my son, I could never have found a better one than Barbara Miller.

Here is my son Tom, a junior high-school student when this picture was made.

This boy has been a shining light in my life. During his early years, my mother saw to it that he was trained in the Christian way. Under her guidance, he developed into a full-fledged Christian.

I had high hopes for Tom when it came to a career. At age eleven, I bought him a flute and he started taking lessons. Caesar Petrillo, the orchestra leader at CBS in Chicago, told me that really gifted flute players were scarce, and that if Tom was a good one, he would earn a fine living in the music field. A prominent orchestra leader heard him play and told me that he had great promise. Naturally, I began to dream of the day when I would see Tom conducting a concert in the Hollywood Bowl and hear his clear flute passages here and there in motion picture musical scores. Knowing a few people in the entertainment industry, I began figuring on various contacts to get him launched on his musical career.

Imagine my horrified surprise when he put his foot down firmly and said, "I appreciate your wanting to help me get started, but I want a different career. I plan to spend my life reaching boys and girls for God through music, teaching good music that will point them toward God."

The announcement floored me. Since my life was practically a spiritual vacuum, I couldn't believe Tom would give up a chance to become rich and famous in the secular music world. But recently, when I heard the celestial strains of Handel's *Messiah* rise from Tom's flowing fingers and swell into the "Hallelujah Chorus," I thanked God that my son had chosen "the better part."

Today, Tom teaches orchestra, glee club, and choir at Los Gatos, California, near San Jose. He has a great influence over young people — he really connects with them.

Tom is a tremendous Christian; in fact, it was through his influence that I found Christ.

Tom and Barbara serve as minister of music and organist, respectively, for the Calvary Baptist Church in Los Gatos. They are shown here with their pastor.

Bedtime for two little girls, Cheryl (on left) and Linda Lou.

As a new stepmother to the three little Rogerses, the going was rough for me at first. But time and experience have taught me a priceless lesson: Any child you take for your own becomes your own if you give of yourself to that child. I have borne two children and had seven others by adoption, and they are all my children, equally beloved and precious.

Cheryl, the oldest of Roy's three, was adopted. Roy told me her story this way:

"After three years of marriage, my wife and I had just about given up hope of having a baby of our own. A friend suggested we might find one to adopt at Hope Cottage, in Dallas. So we went there to look over the babies. After we had seen a few, I stopped by a bed and looked down, and I saw my little girl! I knew instantly that she was the one for us."

Cheryl was a beautiful child. She had honey-colored hair and bright brown eyes and looked enough like Shirley Temple to be her double. And she had been photographed almost as much as Shirley, because Roy and his family received a lot of publicity. Definitely an extrovert, she was everyone's pet. She was interested in everyone, and — true to her Texas heritage — she was always ready to strike up a conversation. Just like me! In fact, I used to think she was like me in so many ways that she might have been my own child.

Within a few short years, we began to realize that Cheryl was no longer a little girl. She still attracted plenty of attention, but now it was of a different kind. When she appeared with us in a show, she began to get a good share of the whistles and applause.

Roy and I were scheduled to do a show at New York's Madison Square Garden, and Cheryl, now in high school, announced that she would go with us. We had to say no because she would have had to miss almost four weeks of school. Cheryl was resentful. She resented *all* authority during those teen years.

While we were in New York, our neighbors across the street back in California had a surprise visitor. It was Cheryl, with her bags all packed. She told them she was leaving home. The neighbor got our pastor on the phone. Cheryl would talk to him because he had her respect and love. He phoned us in New York, and we agreed to have her enrolled at Kemper Hall, an excellent girls' school in Kenosha, Wisconsin.

When we finished in New York, I rushed out to Kenosha. Cheryl and I had a long talk. I think we both felt a lot better after that. She did well at Kemper. In fact, her grades were tops, and in June, when she came home, most of the problems seemed to have disappeared.

As soon as she finished high school, Cheryl wanted to get married to a fine boy named Bill Rose. I pleaded with her to wait a year or so, to get a little college, but it was no use. She had a lovely red-and-white Valentine's Day wedding. Linda was her sister's maid of honor.

This picture is of Cheryl at age fifteen.

Linda Lou was different from Cheryl. She was shy — on the quiet side like Roy. A pretty child, she had blonde hair and big eyes that seemed to speak for her. She shrank from publicity and got very little of it.

At first, quite naturally, the children resented me in the role of mother. One day, while I was arranging furniture in our new home, little Linda Lou lashed out at me. "That isn't your furniture," she said. "It's my mommy's!" I was dumfounded, but fortunately I resisted the urge to reprimand her for speaking her mind. I paused to collect my thoughts and then replied as nonchalantly as I could, "Honey, your mommy has gone to heaven, and she doesn't need this furniture any more. So now you and Daddy and I will have to use it." She didn't say anything more, but my heart was heavy.

I should have known this would happen. Roy was working long hours, and I was there with the children all day. I was a little frightened, I guess, and insecure in my new responsibility. I wasn't at all sure I could cope with all the problems.

Then one day Tom asked a question: Why didn't I start taking the children to Sunday school and church? God could help me do what I was unable to do for myself, he said. I tried it and it helped. Before long, we became a regular churchgoing family.

This picture, taken when Linda was eleven, shows me helping her get dressed on a Sunday morning.

Linda was going steady for some time before we realized that she and Gary Johnson, a former track star at school, were together as much as possible and not dating anyone else. One night, long after she should have been asleep, Roy and I happened to hear her talking to Gary on the phone, and we suddenly realized that their relationship must be getting serious.

But we felt that Linda was too young. She was still in high school, and we wanted her at least to graduate before she thought seriously of marriage. So we sent her off to Kemper Hall, where Cheryl had gone. I won't say that she was happy about it, but we thought it was the best thing for both her and Gary. She made excellent grades, and when she came home for the summer she was quite a young lady. We told her that we were willing for her to marry Gary if they still felt the same way after she graduated. And we promised her any kind of wedding she wanted.

But Linda and Gary were impatient. They didn't want to wait. So they eloped to Las Vegas and were married, with Gary's parents as witnesses.

I was fit to be tied — until I remembered that I had done the same thing when I was even younger. After that, I swallowed my protests and called Roy in New York with the news. He was so upset, he almost broke my eardrums. But I knew it was better to tell him on the phone than to wait and let him find out when he got home. This way, he had a chance to get over his mad before he came back and faced the bride and groom.

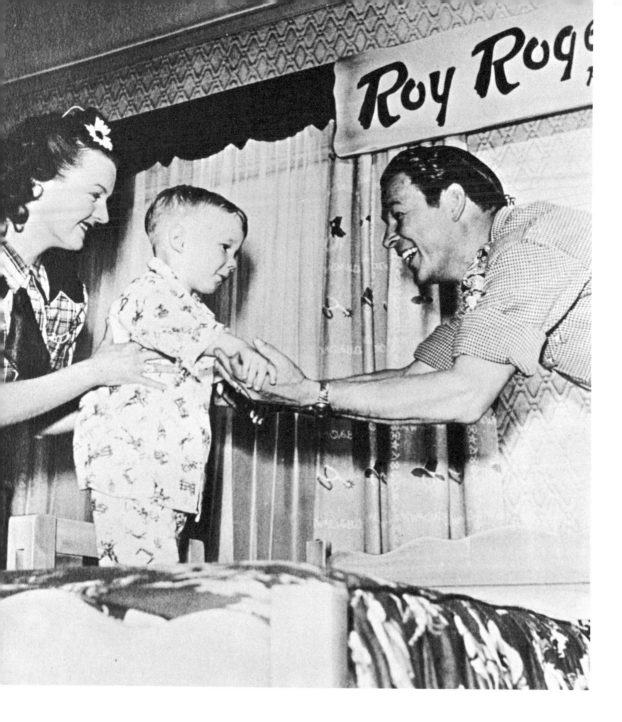

Roy Rogers, Jr. — little Dusty — never knew his real mother; she died a few days after he was born.

When Roy and I were married, we moved into a large, rambling Spanish house in Hollywood Hills, built by the late Noah Beery. There was lots of space, inside and out, with room for dogs and other pets — a good place for a boy to grow.

This picture was taken there, a short time after our marriage.

This isn't a city street, but the back lot of Republic studios, where Dusty and I are shown taking time out for a stroll between shots.

The buildings are parts of Hollywood sets.

The year, 1950.

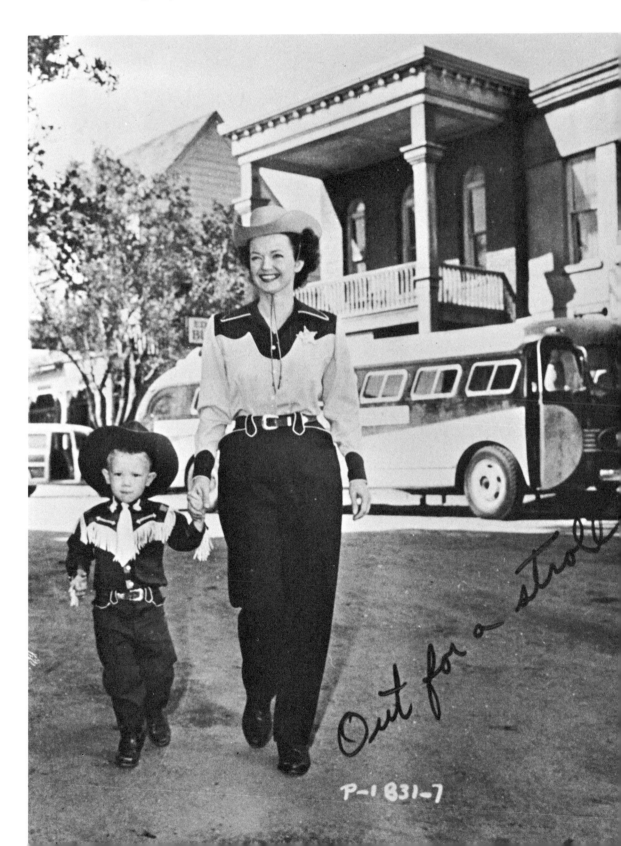

Out for a stroll

P-1 B31-7

If you think this young man (Dusty, age 5) looks like Mr. Mischief, you're right!

Dusty and Sandy (his adopted brother) were a handful for me — so full of pranks that I sometimes swore they had been sent to make my life miserable.

When I went shopping, they'd go along but not to help me shop. They would roll and tumble around in the back seat, yelling like a couple of Apache Indians. Finally, I took to keeping a good-sized switch handy in the front seat so that when they began to get out of hand I could calm them down.

One day, when the switch stung a bare leg, Dusty, as spokesman, informed me, "Mawm, we're going to leave home." I decided to play along. "All right, boys," I said agreeably. "I'll help you pack just as soon as we get home." All was quiet for a few seconds, then he spoke up. "Well, maybe we'll wait a year," he announced.

If there was any trouble, you could bet that Dusty and Sandy were in it. They often worked as a team, with Dusty thinking up the devilment and Sandy carrying it out.

One day Sandy "borrowed" some of Dusty's play money and then swore he hadn't taken it. After a lively chase around the backyard, I caught up with him and administered justice with a peach tree switch.

Another day it was Dusty who made off with unearned wealth. We found his pockets lined with coins that we knew weren't his. Roy and I often left money lying around, and our secretary's cash box looked looted. So we were pretty sure where Dusty got it. We decided that a day in solitary confinement would give him a chance to reflect on his wrongdoing and repent, and he was locked in a dressing room near the swimming pool. He turned out to be a suspiciously happy prisoner. A bread-and-water lunch was to be part of his punishment, but — unaccountably — he didn't object; I thought he almost smiled. (Later, I found out why. The girls had climbed up on the roof and kept him supplied with snacks during the morning.) He never did say where he got the money, but he still remembers his day in jail, and he still talks about it.

I'll never forget the day the two boys decided to inspect the neighbors' mail. They went along the street, shuffling through letters, looking at magazines, and throwing handfuls of rocks at the boxes. I was furious. Brandishing a belt, I took off after them. It was a good chase, and it probably provided a hilarious scene for the whole neighborhood, but I never got close enough to use the belt. I never chased them again!

When Sunday morning came, they would sit with me in church, looking like two little angels. Thinking back, I suppose it was all just part of growing up.

Rusty

After his high-school graduation in 1966, Dusty went to work in a supermarket in Middlefield, Ohio. Roy had hoped that Dusty would stay closer to home — perhaps join us in our work. But Dusty wanted to make it on his own, and we respected that decision.

He fell in love with Linda Yoder, a Middlefield girl. I wept at the wedding — mostly for joy but also at the thought that another one of our beloved children was leaving us.

Seeing Dusty standing so tall and broad shouldered, with his tiny bride radiant in her happiness, brought back a flood of memories to all of us. Our daughter Dodie was one of the bridesmaids, and she was breathtaking in her long, red velvet dress. As Dusty watched her come down the aisle, I thought he was remembering a skinny little girl with dark pigtails who used to play and wrestle with him, and who always stood up for him, even when he was wrong.

It was not easy to let him go, nor was it, I think, easy for him to go. Somehow, nothing ever seems easy for the children of people in public life. There is always pressure, demanding that they conform to someone else's idea of the kind of lives they should lead. We would miss our Dusty, but we were glad for him to have a chance to do what he wanted to do and be what he wanted to be.

So our boy was married. He works today with the Yoder Construction Company in Middlefield, does an occasional personal appearance with Roy at the openings of the Roy Rogers Chuckwagons across the country, and gives Christian witness, along with the showing of a film he starred in which was produced by Youth for Christ.

In December of 1949 I learned that we were to have a child. I accepted it as a miracle, because my doctor had told me that I would never be able to have another baby without extensive surgery.

When I had been pregnant about two months, I caught the German measles. I wasn't very sick, and I had no idea that this might spell danger for my baby. Twice after that I was threatened with miscarriage. Both times I took to my bed until the doctor said it was safe to get up. I wanted this child desperately.

On August 26, Robin Elizabeth — a delicate little blonde — arrived. "Is she all right?" I asked, and someone answered, "She looks okay."

As Roy kissed me, he said, "Honey, she's beautiful; she has little ears just like yours." I was filled with happiness.

But I soon began to feel annoyed because the nurses didn't bring Robin to me as often as they brought the other babies to their mothers. I complained, and received an evasive reply. Avoiding my eyes, the nurse cleared her throat and asked, "Are they going to let you take her home?"

"Of course I'm taking her home. Why shouldn't I?" I asked.

She looked right at me then. "Tell your doctor to tell you the truth about her," she said.

I lost no time calling my doctor. He came, and he told me, gently, that Robin was not responding to some of the tests. At this point, they couldn't tell how she would progress, he said. He suggested that we take her home and enjoy her and surround her with love. "Love will help more than all the hospitals and all the medical science in the world in a situation like this," he told me.

Overcome by grief and too numb even to cry, I prayed, "Lord, I know You understand this. I don't, but I trust You."

Robin's pediatrician told us he suspected she was Mongoloid. His advice was different from my doctor's. He suggested that we put her in an institution promptly, so we wouldn't become too attached to her. She would need a lot of special care, he pointed out. But we refused to give her up. If God had a purpose in sending her to us, we wanted to find it; if we put her away, we never would.

Roy said, "We'll just take her home and love her and trust God for the rest. God will take care of her; she's in His hands, and His hands are big enough to hold her."

I asked our minister, "Why did this happen to us?"

With deep compassion, he replied, "None of us knows exactly why these things are allowed to happen. Only God knows, and if we trust Him, someday we will understand. This experience will cut away the dross and tinsel from your life and you will know, once and for all, what things are really important."

He was right. It was a refining experience for both Roy and me. That refining — the bringing back to basic values — is necessary, I think, if we are to be used of God. He has different ways of accomplishing it. The process is often painful, because the crucible is usually fashioned of whatever we hold most dear.

When Robin was almost two, Cheryl, Linda, and Dusty came down with mumps. Then Robin caught it. The infection went to her brain, and the doctor was grave as he talked to us. He doubted that she would recover, and even if she did, there would be severe brain damage, he said.

The next day, as I was preparing lunch for the other children, I heard the words, "I am going to take Robin." I answered, "All right, Lord, as You will."

In a few minutes she was gone. She was buried on her second birthday.

The day of the funeral, Roy said something that struck a chord deep within my mind: "She looks like a small-size sleeping angel." Suddenly, I thought of a verse from Hebrews, chapter thirteen: "Be not forgetful to entertain strangers; for thereby some have entertained angels unawares."

In a flash, it all seemed so clear. Robin had come to us as a little ministering angel. Through her handicaps, she had taught us that the strength of the Lord is made perfect in weakness. She had taught us some badly needed lessons and helped us recognize the true values in life. Patience, humility, gratitude, and dependence upon God — these were some of the things she had given us a chance to learn during her brief stay with us.

I snatched up a pen and began to write. Finally, after an hour, my hand became cramped and I had to stop. Later, when I tried to write more, I couldn't; it was as if a curtain had fallen over my mind.

Still, I felt that Robin had a vital message. Try as I would, though, I seemed to have reached a dead end. Then one day, as I was praying and turning all this over in my mind, I heard a voice saying, *"Let Robin write it!* You be the instrument. You will be given her message, so get yourself out of the way. Let Robin speak for herself."

After that, the words flowed effortlessly onto the paper. It took just three months to finish the book. It was Robin's — and God's — not mine. He merely used my hand to get it down on paper.

Now I started wondering how to get it published.

Soon afterward, we were filling an engagement in New York. I called Marble Collegiate Church and asked for an appointment with Dr. Norman Vincent Peale, whose book, *A Guide to Confident Living,* had been an inspiration to me. Dr. Peale works on a very tight schedule, but somehow he managed to fit me in.

I told him about the book and asked if I could read a little of it to him.

"Of course," he replied, "but first, we'll pray." On our knees, we prayed together. Then, fighting back tears, I began to read what God had led me to write. Dr. Peale's eyes were glistening. "It's beautiful," he said. "I will help you get it published."

Before long, I had a call from Dr. Frank S. Mead, editor-in-chief of the Fleming H. Revell Company. He asked if he might read my manuscript. When he called and said, "We want it," I wept — this time for joy.

It was as if God said to me, "I took Robin so that you could speak of Me to other mothers with children like her. Robin is safe in the Everlasting Arms. Now you can tell others how she blessed your life in giving you a greater awareness of Me."

Dear, dear Robin . . . Angel unaware . . .

In Cincinnati, Ohio, for a one-night show, we received a telegram from a Mrs. Coleman. With her husband, she ran a welfare home for handicapped children. Their daughter was a cerebral palsy victim, and they wanted her to meet Roy Rogers and Trigger. Roy phoned Mrs. Coleman to bring the child. Then, impulsively, he asked, "You don't happen to have an adoptable little boy about five years old, do you — a boy I could take home as a companion for my son Dusty?" She said there was a little boy of five, named Harry. She would bring him, too.

They came backstage during intermission. Harry was a pale, wistful child — a towhead with great blue eyes just the color of Robin's. His head was too large for his body (due to a bad case of rickets), but he had a ray-of-sunshine smile. When he saw Roy, he held out his hand and drawled, "Hiya, Pahtnah!" Roy fell for him on the spot. He swept him up in his arms and hugged him.

We learned that Harry had been abandoned by his parents who were alcoholics. He was all right mentally, we were told, but his reflexes were slow. Mrs. Coleman thought we could adopt him if we wanted to.

Back in the hotel, Roy and I talked for three hours. Could we really help this little boy become a normal child? Would it be fair to the other children, bringing a second "problem child" into our home after the experience with Robin? Question after question crowded into our minds.

Finally, Roy ended the discussion by saying, "Look, anybody will adopt a kid who has everything going for him, but what becomes of little guys like this one? Let's take him." And so it was decided. A midnight call to Mrs. Coleman set the wheels in motion, and the next morning we appeared before a judge, signed the papers, and walked away with a brand-new son.

The first thing Roy did with Harry was to give him a new name, John David, and a new nickname — Sandy. The second thing was to buy him his very own cowboy boots. Sandy clung to us. He didn't want to let go for a minute. He seemed constantly afraid that once again he would be left alone. Knowing his background, our hearts were torn by his fear.

Back home in California, we asked our pediatrician to examine Sandy. His report was sobering. We learned that Sandy had practically no bridge over his nose. One nostril was almost completely closed off, either from a fall or a blow from a fist. His coordination was poor, and he had astigmatism in one of his eyes.

The pediatrician said, "All I can say is that you've got a lot of guts, adopting a child like this."

Our reply came swiftly, "Let us worry about that. We'll take our chances with him."

We did what we could to build Sandy up physically. His nose was operated on. His tonsils and adenoids were removed. But not all of his problems could be corrected so easily. He had a hard time trying to ride a tricycle. He was afraid to climb to any high place — even standing on a chair frightened him. And he had periodic spells of dizziness and vomiting. He also had enuresis, which was extremely trying for all of us. No matter what we did, he was quite unable to awaken during the night, and each day his bed had to be changed.

We kept him at home until February, and then sent him off to school with Dusty. The two boys had great fun together. Dusty had learned from Robin to understand handicaps, and he made allowances for Sandy. True, he would tease him unmercifully at times, but he was quick to defend his new brother if anyone else tried to do the same.

Sandy was a lovable boy, and we enjoyed him. But there was worry, too. As time passed, it was more and more difficult for him to keep up with Dusty and his pals. When they wrestled, Sandy always lost. He went out for Little League, but he never made a team. At touch football he didn't seem to know when or where to run. Roy tried to teach him to drive the jeep, but he couldn't find the right pedal with the right foot at the right time. With trapshooting, it was the same story. While Dusty was a good shot from the start, Sandy simply couldn't learn to handle the gun. Finally, to avoid embarrassing him, Roy stopped taking them out.

When he was seventeen, Sandy asked for permission to enlist in the army. It was his second request. We had refused the first time, because we wanted him to finish high school. Now, his courage and determination were too strong. "I want to serve my country," he insisted. "I want to prove myself a man." He promised to get his diploma in the service. We gave our consent.

Frankly, we didn't think the army would take him. We expected the physical examination to rule him out, but, somehow, he managed to pass. We thought he would surely be turned down when the facts about his background and his handicaps were known. But that subject never came up, and he was accepted.

Somehow, he got through basic training, and the day he graduated he was on cloud nine. I shared his joy and pride, because this was a real accomplishment for Sandy. He had to fight so hard for everything. The captain of his outfit told me that in his eighteen years in the service he had never seen a boy who tried so hard and was so eager to become a soldier.

Sandy volunteered to go to Viet Nam and was turned down. His reflex actions were too slow. He was assigned to the tank corps and went off to Germany.

It wasn't easy for him there. He made a million mistakes, but his earnest determination won respect from his buddies and officers, despite their impatience with his blundering.

Late in October I went to Texas to visit my mother. When I flew back to Los Angeles, our Scottish foster daughter, Marion, was to meet me at the airport. She was there — and Cheryl was with her. There was an odd look on their faces. Gently, carefully, they broke the news: Sandy was gone!

Losing control of my voice, I shouted, "What do you mean, he's gone? Sandy's in Germany — not Viet Nam!"

Dusty and Roy joined us, and when they had given me a tranquilizer, they told me the story. "Sandy was at a party," Dusty explained. "Some guys got him to drink a lot of hard liquor, and it killed him."

Sandy, who had wanted so much to fight for his country, had been felled, not by an enemy, but by the taunts of "friends" who challenged him to "drink like a man!"

When his body came home, I could hardly bear it. Seeing him there, in his beloved uniform, I was beside myself with sorrow and anger. Sandy had tried so hard to measure up, to prove himself a man, even in a drinking bout!

We miss him terribly. So do the many friends he made everywhere he went. At the Chapel in the Canyon, a bronze memorial plaque captures the essence of his life in these words:

John David (Sandy) Rogers
Here he played. Here he prayed.
Here he loved, and was loved by all.

On our way to New York after Robin died, we stopped off in Dallas. We went out to Hope Cottage, the children's home from which Cheryl had been adopted. Roy thought that seeing the babies might ease our sorrow over losing our own child.

Two months earlier, our hearts had been drawn to one of the babies — a little girl with enormous deep brown eyes, straight black hair, and lovely olive skin. Now we saw her again, and she fascinated me.

In appearance, she was the exact opposite of Robin, who was pale, blonde, and blue-eyed. This child, little Mary, was alert and as vigorous as a jumping bean. She was part Choctaw Indian. Roy is part Choctaw, too.

When I picked her up, her little arms found their way around my neck, and I said to Roy, "This is our child. I want her."

"Are you sure?" he asked. Yes, I was sure. It was all right with Roy.

On the way back from New York, after picking up Sandy in Cincinnati, we stopped at Hope Cottage for Mary (merry little Doe, whom we nicknamed Dodie).

Here she is, all dressed for the trip to her new home.

With the two children, Roy and I boarded the plane for Los Angeles.

The whole family was waiting at the bottom of the ramp when we got off the plane, and press photographers were everywhere. Dodie took all of the excitement in her stride. You would have thought she had spent her whole life before the cameras.

In the fall of 1969, Dodie was married to Tom Faro, then a staff ser-
geant in the United States Air Force. This picture was taken on their
wedding day.

In 1954, Roy and I traveled to Britain to do some shows and give our witness at Billy Graham's London Crusade. On a visit to a Scottish orphanage, we met eleven-year-old Marion Fleming — a tiny child with a haunting voice. She sang for us "Who Will Buy My Pretty Flowers?", an old folk song about an orphan child who is hungry and cold on the streets of London.

We had been away for a long time, and I was longing for home, and for the children. I had missed Dodie's first birthday and was feeling quite low. When Marion began to sing, I almost broke down. We invited her to come to the theater the next day to sit on Trigger and to see the show. She came, and afterwards we took her to our suite for lunch.

We learned that Marion was an orphan of divorce; although both parents were alive, she had been in the orphanage since she was two years old.

We began to think about bringing her to America — just for a visit, of course. We knew we couldn't adopt her, because she was a British subject. Besides, her father had custody of her, and he wouldn't consent. We planned a sort of summer goodwill tour, to let her see Hollywood and have the experience of spending a few weeks in an American home.

Arrangements were made with the authorities, and Marion came. She soon felt right at home in our big family, and when her time was up she tearfully protested that she didn't want to go back. We arranged to keep her until Christmas. Then she begged to stay until school was out, so as not to interrupt her school year.

When summer came, she stayed on. Finally, she became our ward — a permanent member of our international family.

A month after Cheryl's wedding, Marion took the step. This time, it was a home wedding, at the ranch. While Cheryl had had 750 guests, Marion decided on a much smaller group, with less publicity.

Tragedy struck that marriage. Within a short time, the husband, a young Marine, died. But Marion has since remarried.

This picture was taken in 1969.

In 1955 another newcomer joined our international family. She was In Ai Lee, a Korean War orphan.

Months before, Dr. Bob Pierce of World Vision, Inc., had shown us some films that told the story of the hundreds of little ones in Korea left without parents — mostly children of Korean women and soldiers in the UN troops that occupied their country. We had given him a picture of Dodie and asked him to look for a "sister" about her age. Dodie was then three and a half.

When we heard from Dr. Pierce that he had found a child for us, our home buzzed with excitement. Dodie, beside herself with anticipation, prayed, "God, make that man bring my little sister over here soon." The big day came, and six of us — Cheryl, Linda, Marion, Dodie, Roy, and I — formed the welcoming committee. (The boys were away at school.)

Debbie, as we renamed her, could speak a few English words — Mama, Daddy, milk, sleep — but not enough to communicate much. World Vision had given us a pamphlet with a few Korean phrases, but most of the things we wanted to say weren't on the list. At first, Debbie seemed determined to make us learn her language. She would jabber away in Korean; then, seeing our lack of comprehension — she would look exasperated and walk away. When she and Dodie played together, Dodie kept asking, "What you say? What you say?" Finally, Debbie would shrug and turn back to her toys. But once she gave up on Korean, she learned English fast. In a short time, she could speak it fluently.

Debbie was a complete extrovert. As she grew, she made new friends wherever she went. I used to like to sit in the car across from the school and watch her on the playground. She was always surrounded by other children.

The week of her twelfth birthday, the church had scheduled a trip to Tia Juana, just across the border in Mexico. A group of young people, including Debbie and Dodie, were to visit an orphanage there. They would play with the children and take them gifts of clothes, food, and toys. But when the day arrived, Dodie was sick. I wanted Debbie to cancel out, to wait for the next visit, when Dodie and I could go with her. But Debbie was hard to convince. Instead, *she* convinced *me*. Because the trip was part of her birthday celebration, I decided to let her go. Besides, there were plenty of chaperones, and it was an errand of love for orphaned children.

She was so excited. When friends came to pick her up, I had to call her back from the car to kiss me good-bye.

In the afternoon, I went to see Roy, who was in a convalescent home recovering from a neck operation. When I got home, my friend and helper, Ruth Miner, was standing at the kitchen window watching for me.

She looked at me steadily for a moment, an odd expression on her face. Then she took me by the arm and said quietly, "Look, Dale — there's been an accident — the church bus — coming home from Tia Juana. Debbie is gone — with the Lord."

I started to go to pieces. But Dusty — bless him — came in at that moment, grasped me by the shoulders, and shook me hard. "Mom, Debbie is with the Lord," he said. "You've always depended on Him and trusted Him. You'll have to trust Him now!"

Sandy, so overwhelmed he couldn't speak, simply put his hand on my shoulder. There was something in his touch that words couldn't say.

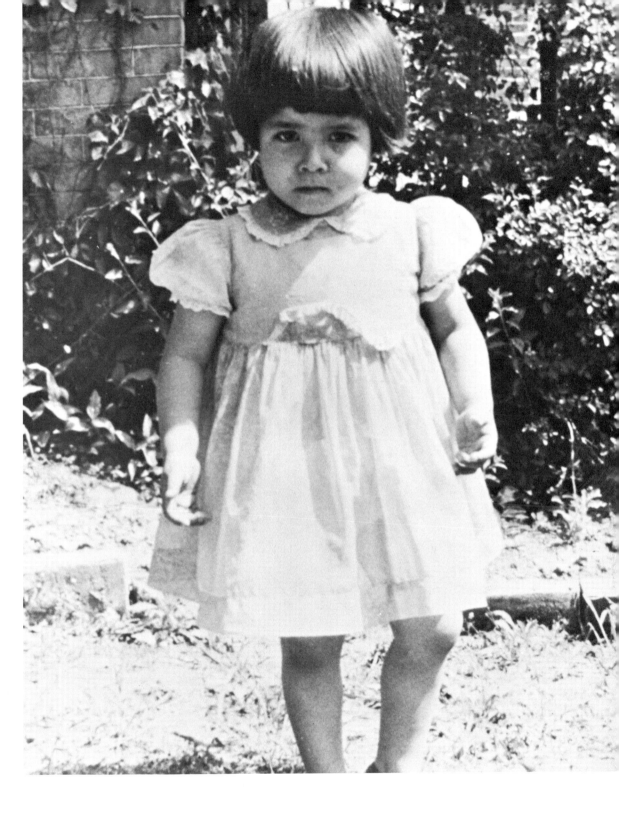

"Our Two Angels Will Never Be Lonely Now"

Somewhere in God's heaven they walk hand in hand now... Roy Rogers' and Dale Evans' two little girls, Robin, who was only 2, and Debbie, the "big sister" she never knew.

Robin Rogers, 1950-1952.

Deborah Lee Rogers, 1952-1964.

A treasured photo, taken only months before tragedy struck, shows Roy and Dale with Debbie (left) and her "twin" sister Dodie, an Indian orphan adopted by the Rogers. The girls were very close.

When Debbie first came to us, Dodie had to make adjustments, too. She had been the baby in the Rogers household since she was seven months old. All of a sudden, she had to share — in fact, to give up more than half of the attention she was accustomed to — because Debbie was new, from a foreign country, and needed lots of help.

We had our moments. Some of them were funny, and some not so funny. But with understanding, and God's love and direction, we closed ranks and became a family.

The two girls, shown here with Roy and me a few months before the accident, had wonderful times together, sharing secrets, hopes, dreams, fears, and likes and dislikes.

Again, I picked up my pen and began to write, pouring out my heart in tribute to a beloved child who had gone home.

The words flowed effortlessly. "You will never be a closed chapter in my book of life, Debbie," I wrote. "You will live in my heart, and I shall go right on singing the Lord's praises until He calls me home, too, to sing in that great choir of the Heavenly Host . . . Oh, yes, my child, there have been those hours, hours of wonder and awe and sadness. I cannot say that I have not wept in sorrow. There was a popular song not so long ago called 'Cry Me a River.' Honey, I've cried a whole sea of tears . . . One day we shall have a great reunion. I'm looking forward to that. But until then, as Stuart Hamblen wrote it in his wonderful song, 'Until then, my heart will go on singing . . . .' "

When the book was finished, we named it *Dearest Debbie* and dedicated it to World Vision, Inc. The royalties have been donated to that organization so that other Debbies might have a chance for a better life.

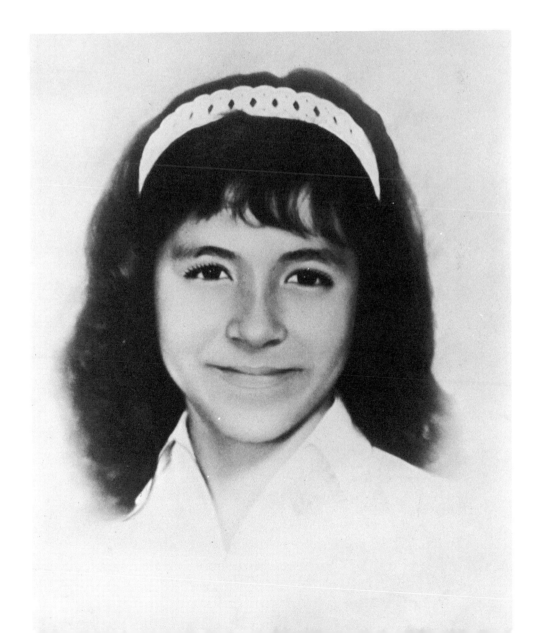

Family Fun

"The water's fine!" How we loved romping in our own swimming pool when we moved out to the San Fernando Valley in 1951! It gave Roy and me an opportunity to relax after long days of work and between out-of-town engagements. Best of all, the girls and Dusty could share in the fun. That was important to us; since Roy and I had to be away from the children a lot, we grabbed every chance to be with them when we were at home.

Our Valley home was a rambling, Spanish-style ranch house. Since Robin was very nervous and needed privacy, she had her own little apartment, built by Roy's father and uncle. Cheryl, Linda, and Dusty had brand-new quarters, with their nurse and our housekeeper next door.

Here on the lawn, with hands joined, are Linda, Cheryl, "Mama," Roy, and Dusty. That's a friend of Cheryl standing near the house.

At eight months, Dodie was more interested in breakfast than in
visiting with Cheryl and me, when we stopped by the nursery to say
"good morning" on the way to church. Dodie had her solemn moments at
this age. She would sometimes make strangers uncomfortable by simply
staring at them, unsmiling. Then, a wide grin would announce that they
had passed the test — she had decided they were all right. She was
quite an individual!

Displaying two new front teeth, little Dodie announces she's tired of posing, much to Sandy's amusement. That's Dusty in the center. Standing behind us are Linda and Cheryl.

"A boy for you, a girl for me," multiplied by two! Here you see Roy and me with the boys, Dusty and Sandy, and another well-known member of the Rogers family, Trigger.

This picture shows Debbie and Dodie listening to a message from Billy Graham. This was in the living room of our house at Chatsworth, where we moved shortly before Debbie came to us from Korea.

Those Special Moments

Here you see my "little brother," Hillman Smith, with his wife, Bennie Merle, visiting me during the forties. This was on the set of one of the pictures I made with Roy. Hillman was just back from Okinawa. He served in the Air Force during World War II as tower-control operator.

Here is Hillman again, with me in the spring of 1947. This was in the living room of my little house in North Hollywood. We have always had great rapport, my brother and I. We understand each other and have lots of fun together.

This is that most special moment of all — when I became the wife of Roy Rogers. From this romantic scene, you would never guess that our life together was beginning under difficulties — a blizzard was raging outside, and the house had just been on fire!

The wedding was on New Year's Eve, at the Flying L Ranch, home of Bill and Alice Likins, near Oklahoma City. The time was set for 5 P.M. Despite terrible weather, all of the guests managed to get through — my parents and my aunts from Texas, Tom and his fiancee, Barbara, and her sister, from California — everyone was there by five, except the minister, our friend Bill Alexander, pastor of Oklahoma City's First Christian Church. Finally, he struggled in through the storm, almost two hours late!

At last, the ceremony was about to begin. With Bill Likins, who was to give me away, I took my place in front of the fireplace. My matron of honor, Mary Jo Rush (wife of Roy's agent and friend, Art Rush) stood beside me. But the groom and best man had disappeared! We waited and waited. Five long minutes passed. Then, just as I began to feel I couldn't stand it any longer, Roy and Art rushed into the room. I didn't know until later that someone had thrown a live cigarette into a trash basket, and Roy and Art had had to stop on their way downstairs to extinguish a pair of flaming curtains.

In the picture, Bill Alexander is in the center. With us are Art and Mary Jo.

Here I am with Dad and Mom, just after the ceremony. (Notice the brooch I'm wearing. It's antique — Roy's gift to me.)

My parents were fine Christians, and they gave me a good Christian home, but I had never managed to make room for God in my life. On my wedding day, I suddenly realized how much I needed Him. I simply didn't feel able to cope with being the wife of a rising star like Roy Rogers. As I thought of him and of the three little children to whom I would be stepmother, I questioned whether I could make it. Reaching out desperately for help, I began to pray, asking God to help me establish a Christian home.

My prayer was answered, and our marriage prospered. Many people who knew us must have been a little surprised; a lot of them had predicted that we wouldn't stay together for more than six months.

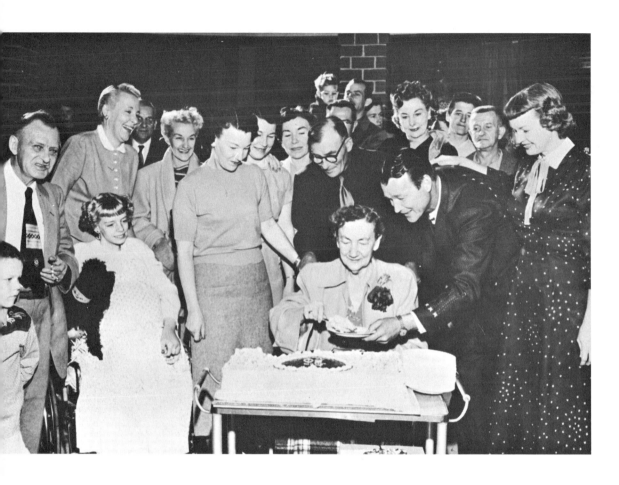

This picture was taken at Roy's parents' fiftieth wedding anniversary. That's his mother serving the cake. She has been crippled most of her life from a childhood bout with polio.

The man standing just behind her is Roy's father. To his right are Roy's three sisters, Mary, Kathleen, and Cleda.

Here we are leaving church on Mother's Day, 1948. Roy's mother is with us. That's Cheryl holding my right hand and Linda Lou my left.

Two little girls in "look alike" dresses get ready for Santa Claus. This picture was taken in the den of our Hollywood home. It was in 1948, the first year Roy and I were married.

The starry-eyed wonder of the children and their eager anticipation brought back cherished memories of the wonderful Christmases I had spent as a child at my grandfather's Texas home.

A year has passed, and it's Christmas again. Here we are with Tom and Barbara, who came to share our holiday joy — and to add to it.

Weddings are always special, particularly when you feel that your child has made a wise choice. Barbara was a lovely girl and a dedicated Christian. We loved her from the beginning and felt that we had truly gained a daughter instead of lost a son.

The bride and groom pose for pictures. At right are Barbara's mother and brother, Mrs. Mabel Miller, and her son, Charles.

Linda tries her hand at a flower garland. This was the first Easter Roy and I were married — 1948. We were at the Toluca Lake Golf Club, where we went for an Easter egg hunt.

Easter again, two years later. This picture was taken at our first home, on the side of a mountain in Hollywood Hills. The grounds were beautiful, with green terraces and magnificent big trees. (This was the spring before Robin was born.)

Most people picture Hollywood as a capital of self-seeking ambition rather than a center of Christian concern. But there are many in Hollywood and elsewhere in the world of entertainment who refuse to make the deadly compromise for success. There are fine, dedicated Christians in show business, just as there are in other walks of life, and some of the most precious moments Roy and I have had were spent with them.

In the early fifties, we became interested in a new Hollywood Christian Group started by Dr. Henrietta Mears, director of Christian Education at the Hollywood Presbyterian Church and head of Gospel Light Press.

Several couples who were active in the entertainment world joined — people who believed in Christ and wanted to be an influence for Him.

Our goal was to live an effective Christian witness, without being overly pious. We wanted to show that Christianity works, regardless of what your employment is. We would talk to others about the group if they asked, but we never clapped people on the shoulder and said, "Brother, are you saved?" or anything like that. We simply tried to live what we believed. If the opportunity presented itself, we talked about the group, and if we knew that a fellow worker had spiritual problems we invited him to a meeting.

Tim and Velma Spencer, a consecrated Christian couple, were live-in host and hostess at HCG headquarters, a Hollywood home rented by the board. They kept the door open day and night for counseling and prayer.

In this picture you see Tim Spencer on the left, and next to him is Dr. Louis Evans, minister-at-large. At the right is Georgia Lee Hoops, who with husband Ralph was under contract to Warner Brothers and made many pictures for the Billy Graham organization. This was a publicity picture, taken in our home, for a big HCG testimonial dinner. Georgia Lee's husband is now an ordained minister of the Gospel.

Beginning with only eight or ten people, the group grew to at least three hundred. It has changed character several times since then, but the seeds are still there.

In 1952, Billy Graham asked me to go to Houston and give my Christian witness at a huge rally in Rice Stadium. I declined, because I didn't want to fly; I was afraid that a crash would leave Robin motherless. Then word came that my father had had a stroke, and I felt that I must go to him. I began to see that it was wrong to put Robin first in my life when God had work for me to do. So I flew to Houston, stopping on the way to see my father.

I have been privileged to testify at Billy Graham's meetings in Houston, New York, Washington, San Diego, and England. With me on the platform here are Cliff Barrows, on the left, and Tim Spencer, head of the Sons of the Pioneers.

This picture shows our family on the day we joined the Methodist church in Chatsworth. That's the pastor, Rev. Harold Hayward, holding Dodie.

We were becoming an international family, and we were an interchurch family, too. Marion was a Presbyterian in Scotland, and she was baptized in the Episcopal Church here. Sandy was christened in the Episcopal Church, and Dusty in the Little Brown Church in Studio City. Linda was baptized and confirmed in the Episcopal Church, and Cheryl by immersion in the Baptist Church. Dodie was also christened in the Episcopal Church.

Sometimes people ask about the various churches we've belonged to. "What *is* your church, anyway?" they want to know. I tell them, "I am a Baptist, Episcopalian, Methodist, Disciple of Christ, and Presbyterian! I don't think of the church as a building or as a denomination. As long as the church fellowship has the seal of the Cross, I'm completely at home there."

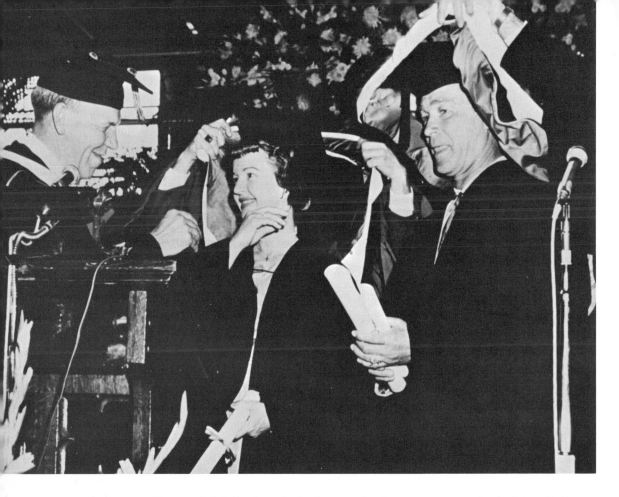

Roy and I felt singularly honored when we were selected by Bethany College to receive honorary doctorates in the humanities. Bethany, the oldest college in West Virginia, is affiliated with the Christian Church (Disciples of Christ) and attempts to provide higher education in an atmosphere sympathetic to the Christian faith.

This picture was taken at Billy Graham's Easter sunrise service in 1956. The service was held on the grounds of Walter Reed Hospital, in Washington, D. C. The morning sky was ablaze with light, and the air was clear and crisp. Roy and I gave a brief Easter testimony and sang our arrangements of "The Old Rugged Cross," "Christ Arose," and "He Lives!"

Another wedding — another special day for the family. Here is the bride, Cheryl, ready to slip into her gown at St. Nicholas Episcopal Church in Encino. Next to her is Polly Chambers, a friend, who made the wedding gown. At right is Mrs. Don Rose, mother of the groom.

Cheryl

Here the bride gets an assist with her veil from Mom.

A new career beckoned Dusty far from home, to Ohio, and there he found his lovely bride, Linda. Our little ones were growing up. Seeing Dodie as bridesmaid, looking so much the young lady in her long velvet dress, Roy and I knew it would not be long before our youngest, too, would be leaving us.

This is December 28, 1969, when Marion married Bill Swift. There are Bill's parents, Mr. and Mrs. Harry Weissberg, with Marion and Bill, and Roy and me. The father of Marion's three children, Dan Eaton, was killed in an automobile accident just before he was to be shipped to Viet Nam as a helicopter gunner in the Marines.

In 1966 I accepted the Texan of the Year Award from Winn Crossley, President of the Texas Press Association. Roy and I both spoke at the San Antonio convention.

This is with my aunt and uncle, Dr. and Mrs. L. D. Massey, in Osceola, Arkansas. In the summer of 1970, Osceola honored him with a fete on "Dr. Massey Day." He heads the hospital there and has given many years of tireless service to the community and the surrounding area. I lived with the Masseys when I was under treatment in Memphis at the age of nine for glandular problems. Dr. Massey attended me when my health broke down at the age of eleven. He and his wife, who is my mother's sister, were really second parents to me.

In 1967, I was named California Mother of the Year. When I went to New York to attend the convention, I was invited to sing on the stage of the "Merv Griffin Show." Here I am singing "What Color Is Love?" I sing it a lot on television because I believe in its message. Dodie, who is part Choctaw Indian, once asked me why her skin is so much darker than mine. I explained that the world is God's garden, where He has planted many varieties of animals, plants, and people. "Wouldn't it be terribly dull in His garden if we all were the same color and looked just alike?" I asked. She bought that.

When my Mom comes to visit us, it's always a very special time. She is more to me than the mother of the year — she gets my vote as the mother of a lifetime! It is true that for many years I rebelled and turned my back on her teachings, but that did not make her wrong; no matter how hard I tried to rationalize and to justify wrongdoing, her example and influence were always there, drawing me back to what I knew in my heart was right.

Regardless of my waywardness, she loved me. She suffered with me in the problems brought on by my foolish mistakes. And she never lost faith that someday I would come to myself and turn back to God's way. Had she lost that faith — I can't bear the thought of what might have happened to me.

Her loving concern extended beyond her own children to her grandson, Tom. It was from her that he received his early Christian training — training that was eventually to lead me to put Christ in His rightful place at the helm of my life.

When Dodie was small, she was scribbling on a piece of typewriter paper one day, doing "homework," she said. Then she showed me her "lesson" and asked, "Mama, do homework say anything?" This is a question we mothers should ask ourselves: Does our homework with our children really say anything? My mother passed that test with flying colors. I hope and pray that I have been able to pass on to my own children the important lessons she worked so tirelessly to instill in me.

In our country, parents' love and sacrifice seem to be taken for granted, while the young in many cultures are taught to be grateful and to show their love and respect as their parents grow old. Why do Americans worship youth and feel that age is a blight? We ought to look at age from the positive angle of development, rather than the negative one of deterioration. As a Christian nation, America needs to take seriously the commandment, "Honor thy father and thy mother."

All in the Day's Work

One thing strikes me when I look back over my professional life — the experiences have been so varied that it has never been a bore! Radio, movies, TV, personal appearances — I've had a chance at all of them. I've played cowgirl parts, sung for soldiers, given religious testimony, traveled to foreign countries, and taken part in parades and rodeos. Life has been unbelievably rich for me, and God has had a hand in making it so. I can surely witness to His power in making my life *abundant* instead of merely *successful*. On these pages, you can see some of the avenues into which this fascinating career of mine has led.

This photo was taken in 1944. I was welcoming an incoming troopship in San Diego for the Hollywood Victory Committee, singing "It's Been a Long, Long Time." It was quite a thrill to see those boys get off the ship and run to greet their sweethearts and wives.

Roy Rogers, a Republic Pictures Star, and Dale Evans.

This is a still for a film Roy and I made in 1949. I was out of pictures for a little while because the studio thought people wouldn't be interested in seeing a married couple teamed up on the screen. But the fans wrote a lot of letters wanting me back because they were accustomed to seeing us together. The fans must be pleased, of course; so back I went.

In this picture Art Rush, who was Roy's manager at the time, had just handed me a contract to read. The year was 1948. Although I had left him in a huff because he seemed more interested in Roy's career than mine, Art and I remained on friendly terms. (Later, I went back to him. I felt a little foolish about that!)

I first knew Art during those years when there was no room in my life for Christian commitment, and he used to talk to me about God's goodness and His ability to guide His children. Over the years, this genuinely Christian agent has been an indispensable source of strength and guidance, and a true friend to both Roy and me.

Roy and I sing out at the Sheriff's Rodeo at the Los Angeles Coliseum (1951).

Those were busy times! Being the wife of a public figure like Roy Rogers; trying to mother the four children and see that our dear little Robin received the best of care; working in pictures, radio, and TV; making personal appearances with Roy — it was all quite a challenge for a country girl.

Sometimes the pressures were almost overwhelming — I felt I must break under them. But then I would realize that God never sends more than we can bear. And with each added burden He supplies the strength we need to stand erect and go on.

Our work has taken us to distant lands. In 1954, we visited Britain, where Roy had a huge fan club. Our purpose was twofold: to meet the fans and put on our show for them, and to help pave the way for Billy Graham's Crusade at Harringay Arena, in London. The press treated us kindly, but it was highly critical of Billy at first. He never replied to any criticism in kind. It was wonderful, the way he used the Biblical "soft answer" to turn away their wrath! And the people flocked to hear him. On the last night, there were 90,000 people at Wembley Stadium, standing in the rain to hear Billy preach.

Roy and I toured the Scottish highlands and visited Robert Burns Cottage. It was on this trip that we first met Marion, the little Scottish girl who later became our ward.

In 1954, Roy and I went to Hawaii, taking Cheryl, Linda, and Dodie. We took a troupe with us, too, and did a stage show in Honolulu. Here you see Roy and me getting off the plane.

Who could ever forget Hawaii, with its fantastic trade winds and incomparable sunshine? In this picture, Dodie and I — still decked in our gorgeous leis — explore our quarters at the Royal Hawaiian Hotel.

Before our show in Honolulu, we spent two weeks at Maui. There we found this extravagant hat for Roy, and Cheryl, Linda, and I took hula lessons for a song-and-dance medley in the show. This picture was taken on stage in Honolulu.

Recognize Roy's friend behind that imposing nose and mustache? I'm all dressed up for a little sequence I did at the Ringling Bros. Barnum & Bailey Circus in Greensboro, North Carolina. The year was 1967.

Here I am in the midst of the World Action Singers from Oral Roberts University. This picture was shot at NBC when I made an appearance on the "Oral Roberts Show." It was a TV special.

Our 1966 trip to Viet Nam wasn't work to us — it was more like a pilgrimage. When the USO asked us to do an entertainment tour, that summer after Sandy died, we agreed, for two reasons. First, we wanted to go as sort of substitutes for Sandy, who had longed to serve his country there. Besides that, we felt a need to find out more about why the United States was engaged in the Asian war.

The Travelon Combo, from Apple Valley Inn, went with us. There were Wayne West, who sings Western ballads to his own guitar accompaniment; Jim Carney on the guitar; Ti Gobert, an ex-Air Force drummer; Roy's cousin Dick Slye, who plays electric guitar and yodels like a Swiss mountaineer; and Charlie Lawyer on the electric piano. (We had to change his name to Chuck, since Charlie is a pretty unpopular name out there!)

We didn't ask them to come. They volunteered. And they splashed and floundered around in the rain and mud, doing two shows or more every day, and never complained about anything. Whether their listeners numbered two thousand, gathered in a big hall, or a dozen, huddled in a mud hut, they gave their best. And they never lacked an audience.

On our first day in Viet Nam, we did two shows. One was in an old rice mill where they had to clean out three feet of rice chaff, dirt, and rubbish before our men could move in. The other was at the USO headquarters, with soldiers standing on the stairs, in the hallways, and in the street outside.

Here you see a soldier presenting me with flowers. (That's Wayne West on my left.) I sang with a big lump in my throat that night. The lump was even bigger when Roy and I cut the ribbon in front of the newly built Roy Rogers Theater.

We had some good laughs, too, though. One night, when Roy introduced me, he said that we had been married almost nineteen years. From the audience, a voice called, "Hey, Roy! Want to reenlist?" I laughed so hard I couldn't sing.

Another time, when our helicopter landed on a muddy field, the gale from the blades caught Roy's brand-new white Stetson hat and blew it halfway across the field. He wasn't amused, but I laughed till I almost cried, watching him chase it, plowing through six inches of mud.

One day, a young soldier said, with a catch in his voice, "Ma'am, I was in Sandy's company in Germany." "Were you there — that night?" I asked. "No, but I wish I had been," he replied stoutly. "It wouldn't have happened." Eagerly, I probed: "He did try to be a good soldier, didn't he?" The answer came without hesitation: "Ma'am, he *was* a good soldier."

This trip turned out to be one of the greatest strengthening experiences of our lives. We worked terribly long hours, but what we did seemed so little compared with what our boys were doing. I came home believing in those boys, and in the cause they were fighting for.

As we turned our faces toward home, we gazed down in farewell upon the land and the people Sandy had longed to help. Soon we were over Japan, looking down on Mount Fujiyama in all its snow-capped majesty. It was strikingly beautiful, and somehow eternal. It made me think of America. So, I thought, stands the undaunted, undiscouraged spirit of the homeland our Sandy loved.

Celebrities

My years in show business have given me a chance to know many celebrities. Here I am with Caesar Petrillo, who was head of music at WBBM in Chicago, in the spring of 1941. This was a program called "Saturday Open House."

In 1942, Don Ameche and I were both featured on "The Chase and Sanborn Hour," with Edgar Bergen and Charlie McCarthy and Ray Noble's orchestra. They were marvelous people to work with. Edgar Bergen is one of the nicest persons I've met in the entertainment world and such a tremendous artist.

Here you see me with Jimmy Durante and Garry Moore on "The Jimmy Durante Show," where I was the featured singer for about a season. This was in 1945.

Of all the pictures I did with Roy, one of my favorites was *Don't Fence Me In*. In it, I pushed Roy into the swimming pool with all his clothes on. That was to get even with him for making me ride in the back of a stagecoach filled with limburger cheese. And he did *that* because I was such a smart aleck. (I played a reporter from the East who was always ready with a cocky answer or wisecrack.)

That's Gabby Hayes with us. This was in 1945. We were a studio family—Roy, Gabby, Pat Brady, the Sons of the Pioneers, and me. I never imagined then that Roy and I would someday belong to the same real-life family!

Easter morning in Washington! On that beautiful Sunday in 1956, Billy Graham (fourth from left in the picture) proclaimed once again the Christian triumph of the empty tomb. The crowd was completely hushed. His voice was the only sound, except for the joyous singing of the birds in nearby trees.

How the world needs Billy Graham! He stands today as a contemporary Noah, John the Baptist, or Paul. And his preaching holds life-giving power for those who hear and heed its message.

DDE

THE WHITE HOUSE

April 2, 1956.

Dear Miss Evans and Mr. Rogers:

I suspect that the excitement displayed by David and his friends at the birthday party Saturday amply repaid the two of you for taking time from your busy schedule to come to the White House, but at the same time I want to assure you that the adults in the Eisenhower family are deeply indebted to you. Your appearance climaxed a day full of happiness for David, in which we all shared.

Mrs. Eisenhower and I join in warm gratitude to you, and the assurance that it was, for us also, a great pleasure to see you.

Since I doubt that David is quite up to expressing in writing his appreciation of the model of the "Bluebonnet," I hope you will permit me to add to this note his delighted thanks.

With best wishes,

Sincerely,

Dwight D Eisenhower

Miss Dale Evans,
Mr. Roy Rogers.

One of the greatest thrills we've had was our visit with President and Mrs. Eisenhower at the White House on the Saturday before Easter, 1956. It was the birthday of their grandson, David. Roy and I sang Western songs for the children (all wearing cowboy hats, of course!). Then Roy gave David a three-and-one-half-foot model of the President's fishing boat. David wasn't swamped with gifts; I was impressed to see that he received less than most people would probably imagine. I thought this was significant. It told me more plainly than words that our First Family was not one that worshiped the material things of life.

After the Easter sunrise service, we went to the National Presbyterian Church where Dr. Elson preached on "Truth Vindicated." He said that two thousand years ago men tried to kill Truth by nailing it to a tree. But Truth arose and has lived through the centuries. It was a powerful message. Here you see us leaving the church with President and Mrs. Eisenhower. Dr. Elson is next to me.

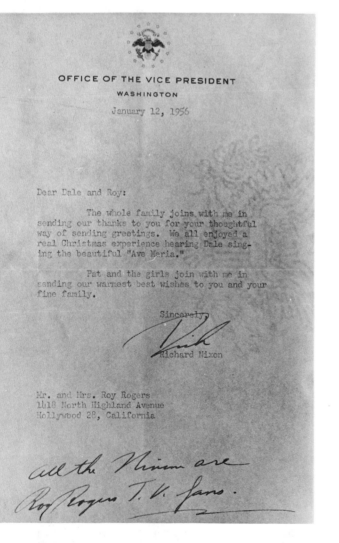

OFFICE OF THE VICE PRESIDENT
WASHINGTON

January 12, 1956

Dear Dale and Roy:

The whole family joins with me in sending our thanks to you for your thoughtful way of sending greetings. We all enjoyed a real Christmas experience hearing Dale singing the beautiful "Ave Maria."

Pat and the girls join with me in sending our warmest best wishes to you and your fine family.

Sincerely,

Richard Nixon

Mr. and Mrs. Roy Rogers
1148 North Highland Avenue
Hollywood 28, California

All the Nixons are
Roy Rogers T. V. fans.

At Christmastime, 1955, Roy and I sent out a personal greeting in the form of a record. On one side was "The Lord's Prayer," sung by Roy. On the other side, I sang the "Ave Maria," with my own lyrics, acceptable to both Protestants and Roman Catholics. Richard Nixon, then the vice-president, wrote us this gracious letter of thanks.

October 22, 1956

Dear Mr. and Mrs. Rogers,

The President and I were delighted to receive your wonderful telegram of welcome to California. Everywhere we experienced a warm feeling of friendly enthusiasm in Los Angeles, and your hospitable message was especially touching.

We are deeply appreciative of your prayers and good wishes for the re-election of the President -- and please express our warm thanks, also, to Mr. and Mrs. Rush for their thought of us.

With very best regard,

Mamie Doud Eisenhower

*Mr. and Mrs. Roy Rogers
Roy Rogers Enterprises
North Cannon Drive
Beverly Hills, California*

When the Eisenhowers made a pre-election visit to California in 1956, Roy and I sent a welcoming telegram, and Mrs. Eisenhower responded with this charming note.

This picture was taken at a Bibletown luncheon sponsored by Mrs. Darlene Swanson, pictured here, and Mrs. Eleanor Whitney. Ira Eschelman, at that time the head of Bibletown in Boca Raton, Florida, had an exhibit at the New York World's Fair.

In this picture, I have just been introduced to a young man with a fantastic singing voice — Oral Roberts' son, Richard. We had just finished one of Oral Roberts' telecasts with singing students from Oral Roberts University in Tulsa.

Our Grandchildren

Mindy

Candy

Julie

Cheryl's Children

Lisa

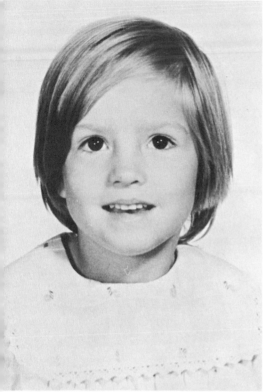

Kim

Brian

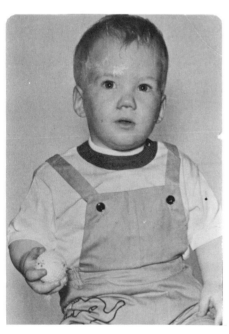

Mark

Marion's Children
Danny, David, Laurie

Linda's Children

Sherry Lee

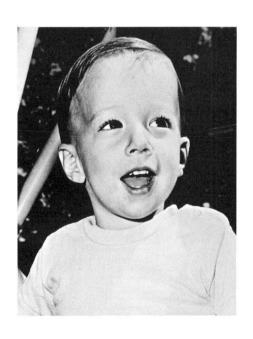

Robin Roy (Robbie)

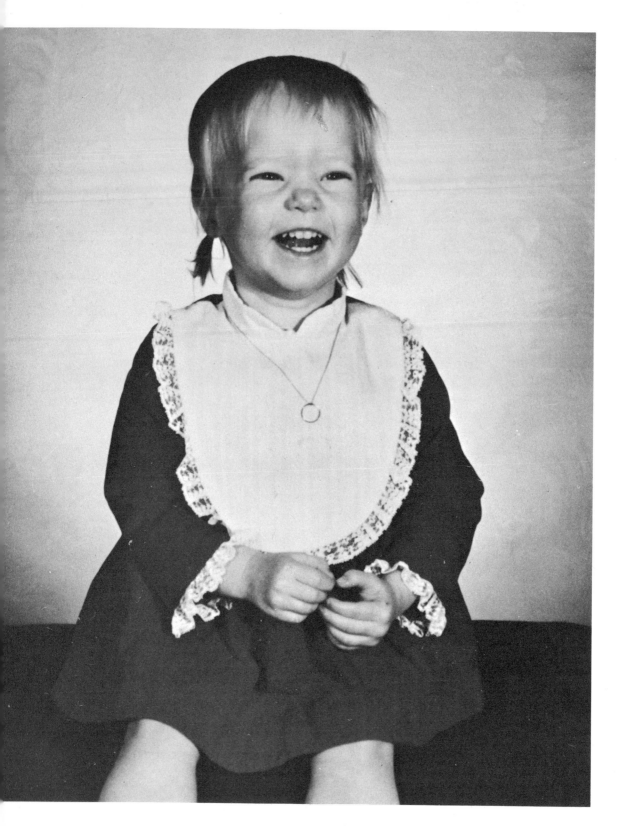

Dusty's Child, Shawna Marie

This is Dodie's one-year-old daughter
Kristin Nicole. Dodie is the youngest Rogers child.

DALE'S AUNT MERLE PULLIAM'S
WEDDING DRESS

CHARLES LINDBERGH

124

Memories! How they crowd in as the years go by! The more we thought about it, the more Roy and I wanted to share our recollections with others. So we bought a big bowling alley and started converting it into a museum filled with photographs and scrapbook materials that tell our life story. There are separate displays for Robin, Debbie, Sandy, and Roy's mother. Another exhibit depicts the religious heritage of our country. Even Trigger is there, standing as natural as life in a room of his own together with his pal, Bullet, the German shepherd dog from our TV series. I couldn't believe Roy was serious when he announced, at the time of Trigger's death, that he would like to have him mounted. But now I'm glad he did. Visitors — kids and grown-ups alike — enjoy pausing to gaze at good old Trigger, recalling the times they've watched him gallop gloriously to the rescue in a Roy Rogers Western.

It's been fun, showing you my photo album and reliving past years. Like most people, I enjoy being nostalgic now and then. But, I remind myself, we must not lose sight of the fact that the past is prologue; it is useful only as a foundation on which we must build for tomorrow. I look forward eagerly to that tomorrow. I am not afraid of the future; I am confident that it will be better than the past because "He holds the whole world in His hand." I rest on that.